Sydney

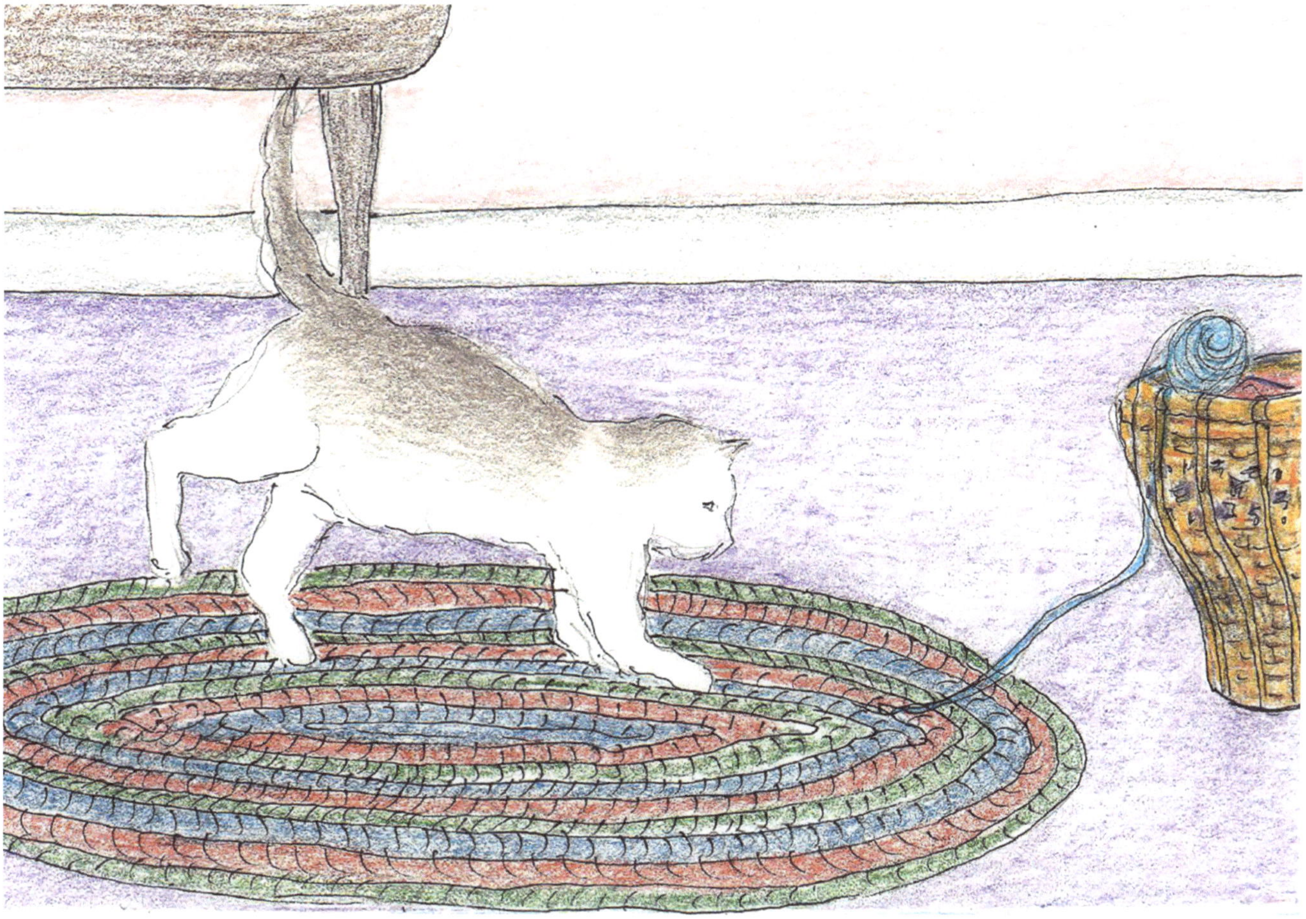

Written by: Diane Baxter Trapeni

Illustrated by: Angela Reed Hinchey

ISBN: 9798601305587

Keep an eye out for these other exciting titles:

Nellie the Nibbler

Alice the Guinea Pig

Penny the Python

Jeremiah, a Song Bird

Vincent

Hubert

Phil Harmonic

Jeff Sticks up for his Buddies

Cord, Glue and 8 Screws

A Three Piggie Circus

DEDICATION

To Ken's sister, Paula, who brought back the piece that was missing to complete the puzzle of our lives. All our love.

DMBT

I want to dedicate the illustrations to the memory of my aunt Minerva's beautiful, white, angora cat, "Baby". I got to know about "Baby" through talks with my aunt and my father's wonderful photographs. AH

Sydney is shy and quiet. She skulks and hides while watching the squirrels gather acorns and the blue jays bickering in flight.

Do you see her?
She's camouflaged underneath
the front porch steps.
Waiting...always waiting...

Sydney spends all her days this way. Watching others playing and frolicking in the autumn leaves.

See! She's watching the blue jays chase each other under the maple tree turned golden and red…

You wonder if she's going to pounce on a bird or chase the squirrels away but she doesn't move a muscle!

She is painfully shy.
She won't interact with the
other playmates in her yard.
It's not that she doesn't want
to...SHE CAN'T!!!

Sydney is literally paralyzed by the fear of opening up to someone.

And she's immobilized by the fear of rejection!

And anyways, she wouldn't know what to say. She never did it before!

Sydney has no "small talk" past, "Hi".
Her mom encourages her to try, so she
practices in front of the mirror, just in case!
But, so far, she hasn't needed to talk to
"them" yet.

Her dad told her to pray about it. That's what he does when he has a problem to solve.
At the end of her rope, Sydney prayed.

"Please help me to talk to someone today." she pleaded.

Every day for a week she said this prayer and every day this week she said, "Hi" to one neighbor. That's 7 times and 7 new friends she said, "Hi" to!!!

Sydney smiles more now.

She has more confidence now.

And…she has 3 close friends now!!!

Just one step...one day...one try at a time and she's licking it. She's not the same kitty she was a week ago.

Now she has plans and goals and someone to share time with.

And she sports a smile that won't stop!!!

She knows that you, too, can do the

same because it WORKS!!!

Sydney wants to hear from you.

Keep in touch.

The End

(of waiting in silence and the beginning of

fun filled days with new friends!!!)

Hubert is Jack's service dog and best friend. They are having their first adventure that eventually leads them all over the world. Let's meet them and tag along.

Also, introducing Joanne Piontec, the magnificent artist. Joanne made Hubert, Jack's amazing service dog, come alive! Hang on tight!!!

My name is Miss Diane. I taught for 42 years and have read thousands of books aloud to children.

I enjoyed that so much, I decided to write and illustrate books for you myself.

Enjoy!!!

Ken Stone Sr. is a computer programmer and a business partner extraordinaire. He put my words, pictures and computer magic together so you could meet, Sydney.